CW00419831

Contents

General Knowledge

1) Who scored Rangers first goal of the 21st Century, in a 5-0 win over Aberdeen in January 2000?

2) In which season did Rangers win the Scottish Third Division?

3) Who was Rangers top scorer in the 2014/15 Championship season with 10 goals?

4) Who made his Rangers debut aged just 15 in a pre-season friendly against SV Lippstadt in 2007?

5) Who became the first player from Mali to represent the club when he signed in July 2018?

6) Rangers secured the 2002/03 Premiership title on goal difference after a dramatic last day victory over Dunfermline by what score?

7) Rangers beat Celtic on penalties to win the SFA Cup Semi-Final in April 2016, but what was the score in the shoot-out?

8) What shirt number has Alfredo Morelos worn since his arrival in 2017?

9) Allan McGregor came off the bench to make his first team debut against which team in the Scottish Cup in 2002?

10) Who was club captain when the club began their season in the Third Division?

11) Who scored a bizarre own goal with an attempted back-pass against Dunfermline in December 2003?

12) Which two Celtic players were sent off as Rangers won 3-2 at Ibrox in March 2012?

13) Kris Boyd scored five goals in one game versus which team in December 2009?

14) Who did David Weir make his final appearance for Rangers against?

15) Allan McGregor saved a late penalty from which player during the 2-0 win over Celtic in April 2021?

16) Who was the main shirt sponsor for the club's first season back in the Premiership?

17) Rangers sealed the Premiership title in 2021 after Celtic failed to beat which team in March?

18) How many league goals did Rangers concede in the 2020/21 season?

19) How many points did Rangers win in their Premiership winning campaign in 2020/21?

Transfers 2000-2009

1) Which Turkish player signed from Galatasaray in January 2000?

2) From which club did Rangers buy Kenny Miller in June 2000?

3) Colin Hendry left in February 2000 to join which English team?

4) Which striker signed from Chelsea in November 2000?

5) Gordon Durie joined which club in September 2000?

6) From which European club was Shota Arveladze bought in September 2001?

7) Who was sold to Arsenal in June 2001?

8) Rangers bought which midfielder from Barcelona in July 2002?

9) Andrei Kanchelskis moved to which side in the summer of 2002?

10) Which two players left to join Blackburn Rovers in the summer of 2003?

11) Which centre-back signed on a free transfer from Auxerre in June 2004?

12) Nacho Novo was brought in from which Scottish club in July 2004?

13) Craig Moore moved to which club on a free after leaving Rangers in 2005?

14) Which left-back joined Rangers from Southampton in August 2005?

15) Kris Boyd arrived from which club in January 2006?

16) Michael Ball left to join which European team in 2005?

17) Which club did Peter Lovenkrands sign for in May 2006?

18) Which English central defender joined from Middlesbrough in the 2007 January transfer window?

19) Rangers signed which goalkeeper from West Ham in July 2007?

20) Gavin Rae moved on a free to which side in 2007?

21) Lee McCulloch was bought from which team in 2007?

22) To which English side was Alan Hutton sold in January 2008?

23) Which midfielder was bought from Portsmouth in August 2008?

24) Which defender was sold to Aston Villa in August 2008?

25) Barry Ferguson was sold to which English team in July 2009?

Cup Games

1) Which three teams did Rangers face in the group stage of the 2000/01 Champion League?

2) Who was in goal as Rangers beat PSG on penalties in the UEFA Cup Third round in 2001?

3) Who scored the only goal as Rangers lost 1-0 at home to Manchester United in the Champions League in 2003?

4) Rangers exited the 2005/06 Champions League after losing to Villarreal by what aggregate score line?

5) Which goalkeeper kept a clean sheet for Rangers in the 0-0 home draw with Barcelona in the Champions League in 2007?

6) Which team did Rangers beat in the UEFA Cup Semi-Final in 2008?

7) Who scored the winner against Falkirk in the 2009 SFA Cup Final?

8) Who scored the only goal in the 1-0 win over Bursaspor in the Champions League in 2010?

9) Who scored the dramatic late equaliser to knock Sporting Lisbon out of the Europa League in February 2011?

10) Who scored the extra time winner to beat Celtic 2-1 in the 2011 Scottish League Cup Final?

11) Which team were defeated in the final of the 2015/16 Challenge Cup?

12) By what score did Hibs beat Rangers in the 2016 SFA Cup Final?

13) Which German team knocked Rangers out of the 2019/20 Europa League?

14) By what aggregate score did Rangers beat Royal Antwerp in the Europa League Round of 32 in February 2021?

Memorable Games

1) Rod Wallace scored a hat-trick in a 6-2 win over which side in March 2000?

2) Who scored the opening goal in the 5-1 demolition of Celtic in November 2000?

3) By what score did Rangers beat Hamilton at Ibrox in November 2020?

4) Who scored the Rangers equaliser as they drew 1-1 with Hamilton in their first game back in the Premiership in August 2016?

5) Who scored four times as Rangers demolished Stenhousemuir 8-0 in September 2013?

6) Who scored the last minute winner in the 3-2 win over Celtic in the 2002 Scottish Cup Final?

7) Kris Boyd scored a hat-trick in an 8-1 Scottish Challenge Cup victory over which side in August 2014?

8) Which team did Rangers beat 4-1 in the first game of the Scottish League One season in 2013?

9) Who scored a crucial last-minute winner against Celtic to secure a 1-0 win in the league in February 2010?

10) Which club did Rangers beat 4-3 in a Scottish Championship encounter in March 2016?

11) Who scored a hat-trick in the 6-0 win over Dunfermline in September 2002?

12) Who scored the only goal in December 2018 as Rangers beat Celtic in the league for the first time since their promotion back to the Premiership?

Memorable Goals

1) Against which team did Kemar Roofe score his unbelievable goal from inside his own half in the Europa League in 2020?

2) James Tavernier scored an incredible volley against which team in the 2016 Scottish Challenge Cup Final?

3) Who scored with a sensational long-range strike in extra-time of the 2016 Scottish Cup Semi-Final versus Celtic?

4) Who won the Scottish Cup in 2009 with his fierce, dipping volley against Falkirk?

5) Who scored in the first minute against Kilmarnock in May 2011 with a brilliant lob to send Rangers on their way to securing the Premier League title?

6) Which defender went on a mazy dribble before drilling in a shot to round off the 7-1 win over Dundee United in December 2009?

7) James Tavernier curled in a long-range free kick away to which side in December 2020?

8) Which centre back scored an outrageous overhead kick to beat Celtic 1-0 at Celtic Park in March 2007?

9) Who secured the 2-0 win away against Celtic in February 2005 with a lob inside the final ten minutes?

10) Ryan Jack teed himself up for a brilliant volley from outside the box against which team in February 2021?

Red Cards

1) Which winger was sent off during the 1-0 away defeat to Hibernian in October 2000?

2) Which two Rangers players were dismissed during the meeting with Celtic in the League Cup Semi-Final in February 2001?

3) Against which side did Michael Mols see red in the Champions League in 2001?

4) Who was sent off twice in a matter of weeks in late 2005, first against Dundee United and then Celtic?

5) Which player was sent off against Lyon in the Champions League in 2007?

6) Pedro Mendes saw red against which team in September 2009?

7) Rangers incredibly had which three men dismissed against Celtic in a Scottish Cup tie in March 2011?

8) Ian Black was sent off during the league match with which club in March 2013?

9) Who was shown a red card against Morton in January 2016?

10) Which Rangers player was sent off four times between August and December 2017?

11) Alfredo Morelos received his first red card as a Rangers player against which side?

12) Daniel Candeias was sent off against which team in the Europa League in November 2018?

13) Allan McGregor was dismissed during the match with which side in May 2019?

14) Which two Rangers players were sent off against Slavia Prague in March 2021?

Managers

1) Who was Rangers manager at the start of the 21st Century?

2) Who replaced Alex McLeish as manager in 2006?

3) Walter Smith faced Dundee United in his first game after returning to manage the club in 2007, what was the result?

4) Steven Gerrard faced which team in a Europa League qualifying match for his first competitive match as Rangers boss?

5) Ally McCoist oversaw a 2-0 home win over which side during his last game in charge?

6) Graeme Murty suffered two heavy defeats to Celtic before losing his job in April 2018, how many goals did Rangers concede to Celtic over those two games without scoring themselves?

7) Who left their job as manager following a 1-1 home draw with Kilmarnock in 2017?

8) Rangers faced Hibernian in the first match under the leadership of Mark Warburton, what was the final score?

9) For how many matches was Stuart McCall the manager of Rangers?

10) Which club was Alex McLeish manager of before being appointed by Rangers?

First Goals

Can you name the club that these players scored their first goal for Rangers against?

1) Ronald de Boer
a) Barcelona
b) Sturm Graz
c) CSKA Moscow

2) Shota Arveladze
a) Kilmarnock
b) Hearts
c) Celtic

3) Tore Andre Flo
a) Celtic
b) Dundee
c) Dundee United

4) Kris Boyd
a) Peterhead
b) Hamilton Academical
c) Forfar

5) Nacho Novo
a) **CSKA Moscow**
b) **Barcelona**
c) **Monaco**

6) Ross McCormack
a) **Dunfermline**
b) **Hibernian**
c) **Motherwell**

7) Kenny Miller
a) **Kilmarnock**
b) **Hearts**
c) **Celtic**

8) Kyle Lafferty
a) **Hearts**
b) **Hibernian**
c) **Celtic**

9) David Weir
a) **FK Zeta Golubovac**
b) **Malmo**
c) **Maribor**

10) Lee McCulloch
a) **Maribor**
b) **FK Zeta Golubovac**
c) **Malmo**

11) Kirk Broadfoot
a) **Falkirk**
b) **St Johnstone**
c) **Dundee United**

12) Nikica Jelavic
a) **Hamilton Academical**
b) **Falkirk**
c) **Hearts**

13) Steven Davis
a) **Villarreal**
b) **Werder Bremen**
c) **Spartak Moscow**

14) David Healy
a) **Motherwell**
b) **Hearts**
c) **Celtic**

15) Nicky Law
a) **Albion Rovers**
b) **Clyde**
c) **Peterhead**

16) Nicky Clark
a) **Brechin City**
b) **Arbroath**
c) **East Fife**

17) Josh Windass
a) **Dunfermline**
b) **Queen of the South**
c) **East Stirling**

18) Cedric Itten
a) **Motherwell**
b) **Hearts**
c) **Falkirk**

19) Alfredo Morelos
a) **Dunfermline**
b) **Celtic**
c) **Hibernian**

20) Ianis Hagi
a) **Hibernian**
b) **Aberdeen**
c) **Ross County**

21) James Tavernier
a) **Hibernian**
b) **Aberdeen**
c) **Motherwell**

22) Jermain Defoe
a) **Celtic**
b) **Dundee**
c) **Kilmarnock**

23) Kemar Roofe
a) **Annan Athletic**
b) **Stranraer**
c) **Kilmarnock**

24) Nathan Patterson
a) **Benfica**
b) **Standard Liege**
c) **Royal Antwerp**

Transfers 2010-2021

1) Kris Boyd left Rangers on a free in July 2010 to join which side?

2) Which striker was bought from Rapid Vienna in August 2010?

3) From which side did the club sign James Beattie in 2010?

4) Kenny Miller signed for which team in the 2011 January transfer window?

5) Rangers signed which defender on a free from St. Etienne in the summer of 2011?

6) Which midfielder joined from Hearts in July 2012?

7) Allan McGregor moved to which Turkish club after leaving Rangers in July 2012?

8) Which experienced goalkeeper signed from Preston in September 2013?

9) Who signed for Ayr after leaving Rangers in the summer of 2013?

10) Who returned to the club, signing from Hearts in June 2015?

11) Which club was Lewis MacLeod sold to in January 2015?

12) Which goalkeeper joined from Swindon in July 2015?

13) Rangers signed which two players from Wigan in July 2015?

14) Lee McCulloch joined which club after leaving Rangers in 2015?

15) Which Swiss defender signed in August 2016?

16) Rangers signed Portuguese defender Bruno Alves from which club?

17) Joey Barton left in January 2017 to re-join which team?

18) Which left-back signed from Cardiff in August 2017?

19) Scott Arfield was signed on a free from which English club?

20) Which centre-back arrived on a free transfer from West Brom in September 2018?

21) Josh Windass moved to which side in the summer of 2018?

22) Who was bought from Liverpool in September 2019?

23) Which goalkeeper left to join St Mirren in July 2020?

24) From which European club did Rangers buy forward Kemar Roofe in August 2020?

25) Jon Flanagan left to join which team in January 2021?

Answers

General Knowledge Answers

1) Who scored Rangers first goal of the 21st Century, in a 5-0 win over Aberdeen in January 2000?
Craig Moore

2) In which season did Rangers win the Scottish Third Division?
2012/13

3) Who was Rangers top scorer in the 2014/15 Championship season with 10 goals?
Nicky Law

4) Who made his Rangers debut aged just 15 in a pre-season friendly against SV Lippstadt in 2007?
John Fleck

5) Who became the first player from Mali to represent the club when he signed in July 2018?
Lassana Coulibaly

6) Rangers secured the 2002/03 Premiership title on goal difference after a dramatic last day victory over Dunfermline by what score?
6-1

7) Rangers beat Celtic on penalties to win the SFA Cup Semi-Final in April 2016, but what was the score in the shoot-out?
Rangers 7-6 Celtic

8) What shirt number has Alfredo Morelos worn since his arrival in 2017?
20

9) Allan McGregor came off the bench to make his first team debut against which team in the Scottish Cup in 2002?
Forfar Athletic

10) Who was club captain when the club began their season in the Third Division?
Carlos Bocanegra

11) Who scored a bizarre own goal with an attempted back-pass against Dunfermline in December 2003?
Paolo Vanoli

12) Which two Celtic players were sent off as Rangers won 3-2 at Ibrox in March 2012?
Cha Du-Ri and Victor Wanyama

13) Kris Boyd scored five goals in one game versus which team in December 2009?
Dundee United

14) Who did David Weir make his final appearance for Rangers against?
Malmo

15) Allan McGregor saved a late penalty from which player during the 2-0 win over Celtic in April 2021?
Odsonne Edouard

16) Who was the main shirt sponsor for the club's first season back in the Premiership?
32 Red

17) Rangers sealed the Premiership title in 2021 after Celtic failed to beat which team in March?
Dundee United

18) How many league goals did Rangers concede in the 2020/21 season?
13

19) How many points did Rangers win in their Premiership winning campaign in 2020/21?
102

Transfers 2000-2009 Answers

1) Which Turkish player signed from Galatasaray in January 2000?
Tugay

2) From which club did Rangers buy Kenny Miller in June 2000?
Hibernian

3) Colin Hendry left in February 2000 to join which English team?
Coventry City

4) Which striker signed from Chelsea in November 2000?
Tore-Andre Flo

5) Gordon Durie joined which club in September 2000?
Hearts

6) From which European club was Shota Arveladze bought in September 2001?
Ajax

7) Who was sold to Arsenal in June 2001?
Giovanni van Bronckhorst

8) Rangers bought which midfielder from Barcelona in July 2002?
Mikel Arteta

9) Andrei Kanchelskis moved to which side in the summer of 2002?
Southampton

10) Which two players left to join Blackburn Rovers in the summer of 2003?
Lorenzo Amoruso and Barry Ferguson

11) Which centre-back signed on a free transfer from Auxerre in June 2004?
Jean-Alain Boumsong

12) Nacho Novo was brought in from which Scottish club in July 2004?
Dundee

13) Craig Moore moved to which club on a free after leaving Rangers in 2005?
Borussia Monchengladbach

14) Which left-back joined Rangers from Southampton in August 2005?
Olivier Bernard

15) Kris Boyd arrived from which club in January 2006?
Kilmarnock

16) Michael Ball left to join which European team in 2005?
PSV Eindhoven

17) Which club did Peter Lovenkrands sign for in May 2006?
Schalke

18) Which English central defender joined from Middlesbrough in the 2007 January transfer window?
Ugo Ehiogu

19) Rangers signed which goalkeeper from West Ham in July 2007?
Roy Carroll

20) Gavin Rae moved on a free to which side in 2007?
Cardiff City

21) Lee McCulloch was bought from which team in 2007?
Wigan Athletic

22) To which English side was Alan Hutton sold in January 2008?
Tottenham Hotspur

23) Which midfielder was bought from Portsmouth in August 2008?
Pedro Mendes

24) Which defender was sold to Aston Villa in August 2008?
Carlos Cuellar

25) Barry Ferguson was sold to which English team in July 2009?
Birmingham City

Cup Games Answers

1) Which three teams did Rangers face in the group stage of the 2000/01 Champion League?
Sturm Graz, Monaco and Galatasaray

2) Who was in goal as Rangers beat PSG on penalties in the UEFA Cup Third round in 2001?
Stefan Klos

3) Who scored the only goal as Rangers lost 1-0 at home to Manchester United in the Champions League in 2003?
Phil Neville

4) Rangers exited the 2005/06 Champions League after losing to Villarreal by what aggregate score line?
3-3

5) Which goalkeeper kept a clean sheet for Rangers in the 0-0 home draw with Barcelona in the Champions League in 2007?
Allan McGregor

6) Which team did Rangers beat in the UEFA Cup Semi-Final in 2008?
Fiorentina

7) Who scored the winner against Falkirk in the 2009 SFA Cup Final?
Nacho Novo

8) Who scored the only goal in the 1-0 win over Bursaspor in the Champions League in 2010?
Steven Naismith

9) Who scored the dramatic late equaliser to knock Sporting Lisbon out of the Europa League in February 2011?
Maurice Edu

10) Who scored the extra time winner to beat Celtic 2-1 in the 2011 Scottish League Cup Final?
Nikica Jelavic

11) Which team were defeated in the final of the 2015/16 Challenge Cup?
Peterhead

12) By what score did Hibs beat Rangers in the 2016 SFA Cup Final?
3-2

13) Which German team knocked Rangers out of the 2019/20 Europa League?
Bayer Leverkusen

14) By what aggregate score did Rangers beat Royal Antwerp in the Europa League Round of 32 in February 2021?
9-5

Memorable Games Answers

1) Rod Wallace scored a hat-trick in a 6-2 win over which side in March 2000?
Motherwell

2) Who scored the opening goal in the 5-1 demolition of Celtic in November 2000?
Barry Ferguson

3) By what score did Rangers beat Hamilton at Ibrox in November 2020?
8-0

4) Who scored the Rangers equaliser as they drew 1-1 with Hamilton in their first game back in the Premiership in August 2016?
Martyn Waghorn

5) Who scored four times as Rangers demolished Stenhousemuir 8-0 in September 2013?
Jon Daly

6) Who scored the last minute winner in the 3-2 win over Celtic in the 2002 Scottish Cup Final?
Peter Lovenkrands

7) Kris Boyd scored a hat-trick in an 8-1 Scottish Challenge Cup victory over which side in August 2014?
Clyde

8) Which team did Rangers beat 4-1 in the first game of the Scottish League One season in 2013?
Brechin City

9) Who scored a crucial last-minute winner against Celtic to secure a 1-0 win in the league in February 2010?
Maurice Edu

10) Which club did Rangers beat 4-3 in a Scottish Championship encounter In March 2016?
Queen of the South

11) Who scored a hat-trick in the 6-0 win over Dunfermline in September 2002?
Claudio Caniggia

12) Who scored the only goal in December 2018 as Rangers beat Celtic in the league for the first time since their promotion back to the Premiership?
Ryan Jack

Memorable Goals Answers

1) Against which team did Kemar Roofe score his unbelievable goal from inside his own half in the Europa League in 2020?
Standard Liege

2) James Tavernier scored an incredible volley against which team in the 2016 Scottish Challenge Cup Final?
Peterhead

3) Who scored with a sensational long-range strike in extra-time of the 2016 Scottish Cup Semi-Final versus Celtic?
Barrie McKay

4) Who won the Scottish Cup in 2009 with his fierce, dipping volley against Falkirk?
Nacho Novo

5) Who scored in the first minute against Kilmarnock in May 2011 with a brilliant lob to send Rangers on their way to securing the Premier League title?
Kyle Lafferty

6) Which defender went on a mazy dribble before drilling in a shot to round off the 7-1 win over Dundee United in December 2009?
Madjid Bougherra

7) James Tavernier curled in a long-range free kick away to which side in December 2020?
Dundee United

8) Which centre back scored an outrageous overhead kick to beat Celtic 1-0 at Celtic Park in March 2007?
Ugo Ehiogu

9) Who secured the 2-0 win away against Celtic in February 2005 with a lob inside the final ten minutes?

Nacho Novo

10) Ryan Jack teed himself up for a brilliant volley from outside the box against which team in February 2021?

Kilmarnock

Red Cards Answers

1) Which winger was sent off during the 1-0 away defeat to Hibernian in October 2000?
Andrei Kanchelskis

2) Which two Rangers players were dismissed during the meeting with Celtic in the League Cup Semi-Final in February 2001?
Claudio Reyna and Michael Mols

3) Against which side did Michael Mols see red in the Champions League in 2001?
Fenerbahce

4) Who was sent off twice in a matter of weeks in late 2005, first against Dundee United and then Celtic?
Sotirios Kyrgiakos

5) Which player was sent off against Lyon in the Champions League in 2007?
Jean Claude Darcheville

6) Pedro Mendes saw red against which team in September 2009?
Kilmarnock

7) Rangers incredibly had which three men dismissed against Celtic in a Scottish Cup tie in March 2011?
Steven Whittaker, Madjid Bougherra and El Hadji Diouf

8) Ian Black was sent off during the league match with which club in March 2013?
Elgin City

9) Who was shown a red card against Morton in January 2016?
Andy Halliday

10) Which Rangers player was sent off four times between August and December 2017?
Ryan Jack

11) Alfredo Morelos received his first red card as a Rangers player against which side?
Aberdeen

12) Daniel Candeias was sent off against which team in the Europa League in November 2018?
Villarreal

13) Allan McGregor was dismissed during the match with which side in May 2019?
Hibernian

14) Which two Rangers players were sent off against Slavia Prague in March 2021?
Kemar Roofe and Leon Balogun

Managers Answers

1) Who was Rangers manager at the start of the 21st Century?
Dick Advocaat

2) Who replaced Alex McLeish as manager in 2006?
Paul Le Guen

3) Walter Smith faced Dundee United in his first game after returning to manage the club in 2007, what was the result?
Rangers 5-0 Dundee United

4) Steven Gerrard faced which team in a Europa League qualifying match for his first competitive match as Rangers boss?
FC Shkupi

5) Ally McCoist oversaw a 2-0 home win over which side during his last game in charge?
Livingston

6) Graeme Murty suffered two heavy defeats to Celtic before losing his job in April 2018, how many goals did Rangers concede to Celtic over those two games without scoring themselves?

9

7) Who left their job as manager following a 1-1 home draw with Kilmarnock in 2017?

Pedro Caixinha

8) Rangers faced Hibernian in the first match under the leadership of Mark Warburton, what was the final score?

Hibernian 2-6 Rangers

9) For how many matches was Stuart McCall the manager of Rangers?

15

10) Which club was Alex McLeish manager of before being appointed by Rangers?

Hibernian

First Goals Answers

1) Ronald de Boer
   Sturm Graz

2) Shota Arveladze
   Kilmarnock

3) Tore Andre Flo
   Celtic

4) Kris Boyd
   Peterhead

5) Nacho Novo
   CSKA Moscow

6) Ross McCormack
   Dunfermline

7) Kenny Miller
   Kilmarnock

8) Kyle Lafferty
   Hearts

9) David Weir
   FK Zeta Golubovac

10) Lee McCulloch
    FK Zeta Golubovac

11) Kirk Broadfoot
    Falkirk

12) Nikica Jelavic
    Hamilton Academical

13) Steven Davis
    Werder Bremen

14) David Healy
    Motherwell

15) Nicky Law
    Albion Rovers

16) Nicky Clark
    East Fife

17) Josh Windass
East Stirling

18) Cedric Itten
Motherwell

19) Alfredo Morelos
Dunfermline

20) Ianis Hagi
Hibernian

21) James Tavernier
Hibernian

22) Jermain Defoe
Kilmarnock

23) Kemar Roofe
Kilmarnock

24) Nathan Patterson
Royal Antwerp

Transfers 2010-2021 Answers

1) Kris Boyd left Rangers on a free in July 2010 to join which side?
Middlesbrough

2) Which striker was bought from Rapid Vienna in August 2010?
Nikica Jelavic

3) From which side did the club sign James Beattie in 2010?
Stoke City

4) Kenny Miller signed for which team in the 2011 January transfer window?
Bursaspor

5) Rangers signed which defender on a free from St. Etienne in the summer of 2011?
Carlos Bocanegra

6) Which midfielder joined from Hearts in July 2012?
Ian Black

7) Allan McGregor moved to which Turkish club after leaving Rangers in July 2012?
Besiktas

8) Which experienced goalkeeper signed from Preston in September 2013?
Steve Simonsen

9) Who signed for Ayr after leaving Rangers in the summer of 2013?
Kevin Kyle

10) Who returned to the club, signing from Hearts in June 2015?
Danny Wilson

11) Which club was Lewis MacLeod sold to in January 2015?
Brentford

12) Which goalkeeper joined from Swindon in July 2015?
Wes Foderingham

13) Rangers signed which two players from Wigan in July 2015?
Martyn Waghorn and James Tavernier

14) Lee McCulloch joined which club after leaving Rangers in 2015?
Kilmarnock

15) Which Swiss defender signed in August 2016?
Philippe Senderos

16) Rangers signed Portuguese defender Bruno Alves from which club?
Cagliari

17) Joey Barton left in January 2017 to re-join which team?
Burnley

18) Which left-back signed from Cardiff in August 2017?

Declan John

19) Scott Arfield was signed on a free from which English club?

Burnley

20) Which centre-back arrived on a free transfer from West Brom in September 2018?

Gareth McAuley

21) Josh Windass moved to which side in the summer of 2018?

Wigan

22) Who was bought from Liverpool in September 2019?

Ryan Kent

23) Which goalkeeper left to join St Mirren in July 2020?

Jak Alnwick

24) From which European club did Rangers buy forward Kemar Roofe in August 2020?

Anderlecht

25) Jon Flanagan left to join which team in January 2021?

Charleroi

If you enjoyed this book please consider leaving a five star review on Amazon

Books by Jack Pearson available on Amazon:

Cricket:

Cricket World Cup 2019 Quiz Book
The Ashes 2019 Cricket Quiz Book
The Ashes 2010-2019 Quiz Book
The Ashes 2005 Quiz Book
The Indian Premier League Quiz Book

Football:

The Quiz Book of the England Football Team in the 21st Century
The Quiz Book of Arsenal Football Club in the 21st Century
The Quiz Book of Aston Villa Football Club in the 21st Century
The Quiz Book of Chelsea Football Club in the 21st Century

The Quiz Book of Everton Football Club in the 21st Century

The Quiz Book of Leeds United Football Club in the 21st Century

The Quiz Book of Leicester City Football Club in the 21st Century

The Quiz Book of Liverpool Football Club in the 21st Century

The Quiz Book of Manchester City Football Club in the 21st Century

The Quiz Book of Manchester United Football Club in the 21st Century

The Quiz Book of Newcastle United Football Club in the 21st Century

The Quiz Book of Southampton Football Club in the 21st Century

The Quiz Book of Sunderland Association Football Club in the 21st Century

The Quiz Book of Tottenham Hotspur Football Club in the 21st Century

The Quiz Book of West Ham United Football Club in the 21st Century

The Quiz Book of Wrexham Association Football Club in the 21st Century

Printed in Great Britain
by Amazon